Walk Around

de Havilland Mosquito

By Ron MacKay

Color by Don Greer

Illustrated by Richard Hudson

Walk Around Number 15

squadron/signal publications

Introduction

This project began in positive fashion, was blunted for some time by a tragic turn of fate, and finally brought to maturity. My initial attention had been concentrated on the Mosquito Air Museum which possesses not only a late model 'Mossie' B Mk 35, but also W4050 — the original prototype for De Havilland's superb 'Wooden Wonder'. Access to the T Mk III (with which to illustrate the fighter version of the Mosquito) operated in flying condition by British Aerospace had been provisionally agreed upon when the aircraft and its two-man crew were lost in an airshow accident. Fortunately an alternative source subsequently came to light with a visit to the Yorkshire Air Museum where Tony Agar's Mosquito had been patiently constructed (literally from nothing) over many years. Although only a portion of the overall airframe is vintage NF Mk II, the aircraft provided sufficient detail to outline the De Havilland design as intended to operate in a fighter-bomber role.

The Mosquito will always hold a place of great affection in the minds of all those who either flew her in combat during World War Two, or who have an interest in the conduct of that conflict. Along with the Spitfire, Hurricane, and Lancaster, the Mosquito completes the quartet of truly preeminent British military aircraft whose marriage to the Rolls-Royce Merlin aero-engine granted the RAF a platform with which to properly and fully prosecute the war in the air.

Acknowledgements

Many thanks to the staff of the Mosquito Air Museum for permitting unlimited access to their collection of preserved Mosquitos. My thanks are also directed specifically to Ian Thirsk, Ron Ayres, and Bruce Gordon for their assistance on all technical matters. Equal gratitude is expressed to Tony Agar at the Yorkshire Air Museum — his assistance in photographing the NF Mk II was to prove particularly invaluable. Colin Francis provided superb photographic results as ever.

PHOTO CREDITS

Bruce Robertson
J D R Rawlings
Jerry Scutts
Martin Bowman
Steve Adams
Mike Bailey
Imperial War Museum (IWM)

ISBN 0-89747-396-5

If you have any photographs of aircraft, armor, soldiers or ships of any nation, particularly wartime snapshots, why not share them with us and help make Squadron/Signal's books all the more interesting and complete in the future. Any photograph sent to us will be copied and the original returned. The donor will be fully credited for any photos used. Please send them to:

Squadron/Signal Publications, Inc.
1115 Crowley Drive
Carrollton, TX 75011-5010

Если у вас есть фотографии самолётов, вооружения, солдат или кораблей любой страны, особенно, снимки времён войны, поделитесь с нами и помогите сделать новые книги издательства Эскадрон/Сигнал ещё интереснее. Мы переснимем ваши фотографии и вернём оригиналы. Имена приславших снимки будут сопровождать все опубликованные фотографии. Пожалуйста, присылайте фотографии по адресу:

Squadron/Signal Publications, Inc.
1115 Crowley Drive
Carrollton, TX 75011-5010

軍用機、装甲車両、兵士、軍艦などの写真を所持しておられる方はいらっしゃいませんか？どの国のものでも結構です。作戦中に撮影されたものが特に良いのです。Squadron/Signal社の出版する刊行物において、このような写真は内容を一層充実し、興味深くすることができます。当方にお送り頂いた写真は、複写の後お返しいたします。出版物中に写真を使用した場合は、必ず提供者のお名前を明記させて頂きます。お写真は下記にご送付ください。

Squadron/Signal Publications, Inc.
1115 Crowley Drive
Carrollton, TX 75011-5010

(Previous Page) A Mosquito NF II (DD739) cruises between layers of cloud sometime during 1943. The aircraft was assigned to No. 456 Squadron which was re-equipped with Mosquito NF IIs in late 1942. Mosquito DD739 was lost on a bomber support mission to Kassel, Germany on 4 December 1943.

(Front Cover) Mosquito FB VI (SD*V/MM403) of No. 464 Squadron, RAF roars past a smoking Fw 190 during low level intruder operations behind the Normandy beaches in June of 1944. This aircraft had also taken part in the famous attack on Amiens Prison to free resistance personnel captured by the Germans. MM403 was lost on the night of 17 January 1945.

(Back Cover) Mosquito NF II (RS*B/W4087) of No. 157 Squadron, RAF is prepared for a night mission shortly before dusk in late May of 1941. No. 157 Squadron is believed to be the first RAF night fighter unit to operate all black Mosquitos in the night fighter role.

The Mosquito prototype (W4050) was first flown on 25 November 1940. The prototype was used as a trials aircraft and went through several modifications during World War II. It is now retired to the Mosquito Museum at Salisbury Hall north of London.

Mosquito Prototype

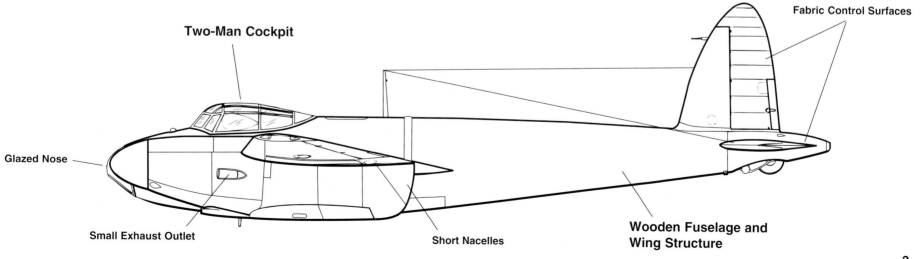

Two-Man Cockpit

Fabric Control Surfaces

Glazed Nose

Small Exhaust Outlet

Short Nacelles

Wooden Fuselage and Wing Structure

Early variants of the Mosquito were equipped with single stage Merlin engines and a slim cowl. Early Mosquitos used needle-bladed propellers, while later variants used the paddle-bladed units depicted here. W4050 is also fitted with a blunter Lancaster type spinner.

The main landing gear of W4050 consists of two vertical De Havilland compression struts linked by a series of cross braces above the wheel. The tire is mounted on a tubular steel axle joined at the lower end of the compression struts. The entire unit folds back into the engine nacelle. The landing gear struts were normally painted silver.

4

The landing gear shock absorbers were rather unusual. The oval steel strut contained a series of eleven and a half rubber blocks and spacers, a bakelite piston, a rebound rubber block, and the telescoping strut. No hydro-pneumatic systems were involved. This system was used on all Mosquito variants except the Sea Mosquito which reverted to a standard hydraulic system for carrier deck landings.

The Mosquito prototype was fitted with flame dampening exhaust shrouds during her career. The small duct on top of the shroud directs cooling air to the exhaust manifold, while the lower row of slots performs a similar function for the ends of the exhausts.

The bulge on the port side of the engine cowl covers part of the engine coolant pipe. Just behind and below the exhaust is the Inconel heat resistant panel used to protect the nacelle skin from the Merlin engine's exhaust. It is formed from a titanium-based metal. The fuel pipe cooling duct is in line with the end of the shroud.

The Merlin engine used an updraft carburetor which required the placement of the carburetor air intake below the engine cowling. Single stage supercharged Merlin engines used a small air intake mounted midway along the bottom of the cowl. The mesh ice guard was an optional fitting.

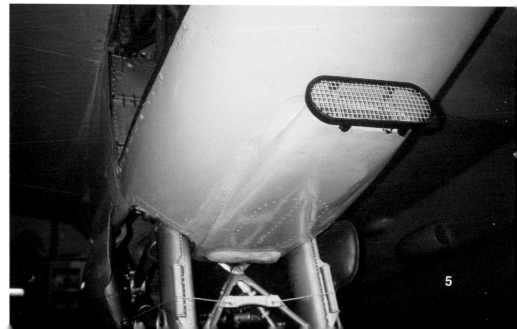

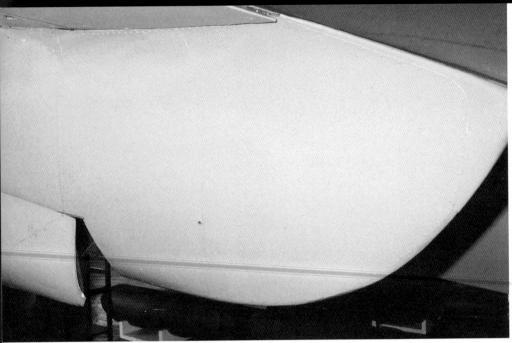

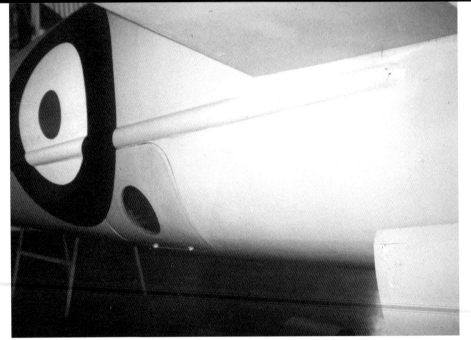

The original engine nacelles did not extend beyond the trailing edge of the wing. The short nacelles were used on Mosquito B Mk I and PR I aircraft, but were lengthened to improve air flow and lessen buffeting around the tail. Long nacelles were used on all later Mosquito variants.

Five elbow hinges are used to attach the bomb bay doors to the fuselage. The air scoop provides cooling air for the center fuel tanks.

W4050's starboard rear fuselage was strengthened with a strake following a fracture during testing. The strake was added to all subsequent Mosquito variants. The hatch provided access to the aft fuselage. The window in the harch was used for flight testing and did not appear on production aircraft.

The elbow-shaped bomb bay door hinges pushed the door away from the fuselage as it opened. The interior of the bomb bay was painted grey-green (FS 34226). The bomb bay was designed for four 250 lb bombs. Later variants carried four 500 lb bombs. The larger bombs had shorter fins in order to fit within the bomb bay.

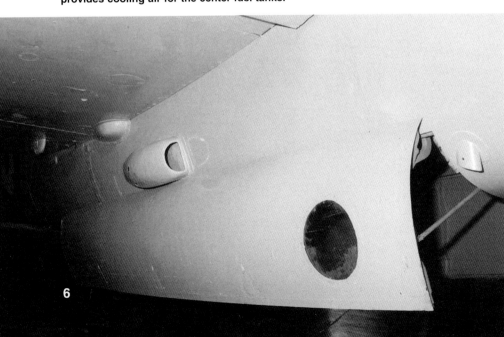

The bomb bay held two 70 gallon pressurized fuel tanks. A common collector box fed fuel to either or both engines. The tanks could also feed each other — for balance purposes — via the cross-feed pipes between the center and rear retaining straps.

W4050 carries the radio antenna attachment point further down on the leading edge than standard production aircraft. The location of the pitot tube remained standard on all production Mosquitos.

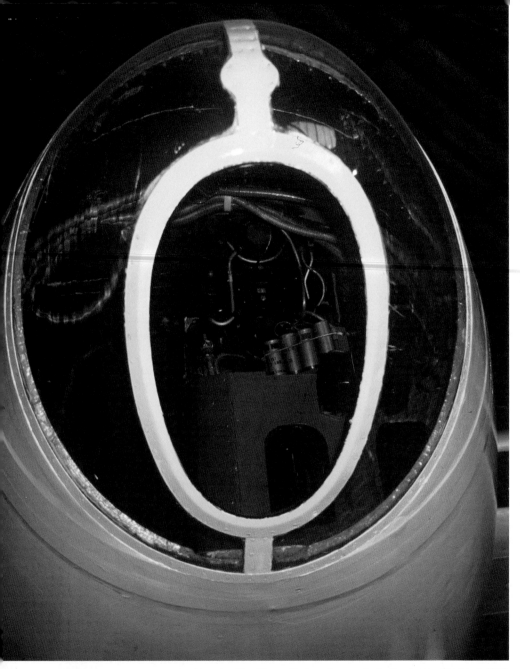

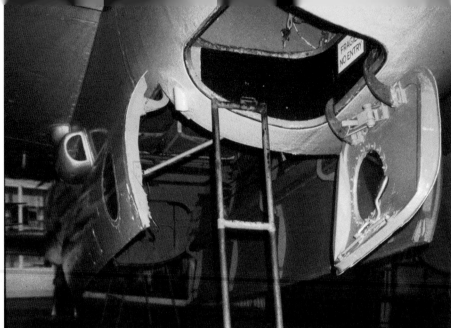

Entrance to bomber and PR Mosquitos was gained through a hatch located on the starboard side of the fuselage directly under the cockpit floor. A telescoping metal ladder was stored in a compartment in front of the hatch door.

The interior canopy framing was formed from metal tubes. An escape hatch was set into the center of the upper panel. A single release lever pulled a cable running around the periphery of the hatch, opening the latches, and jettisoning the hatch. The interior of the canopy frames was painted grey-green.

A perspex nose was common on the Mosquito bomber and photo-reconnaissance (PR) versions. The thick vertical reinforcing frame attached to the oval optical flat was replaced by a thinner version on later variants.

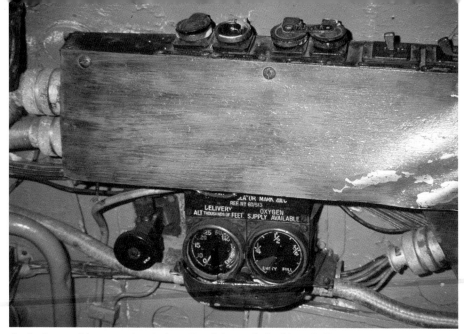

An instrument box was located on the right cockpit sidewall. The box contained the red engine fire extinguisher switches and the IFF detonator buttons. Oxygen monitoring dials are mounted under the electrical box. The prototype does not have a complete cockpit.

The rudder pedals were suspended from hinged tubes located behind the instrument panel. These pedals have the metal footrests replaced by wooden blocks. The footrests could be adjusted fore-and-aft by moving them from one slot to another. The pedals were normally painted grey-green.

Mosquito bomber and photo-reconnaissance (PR) versions were equipped with a control column and wheel. The lever and thumb button control the brakes. The elevator control tube (not visible) extends from the base of the column. The circular compass binnacle is mounted on the left cockpit sidewall, while the throttle quadrant is mounted above and behind it. The cockpit interior was painted grey-green.

9

Mosquito FB VI

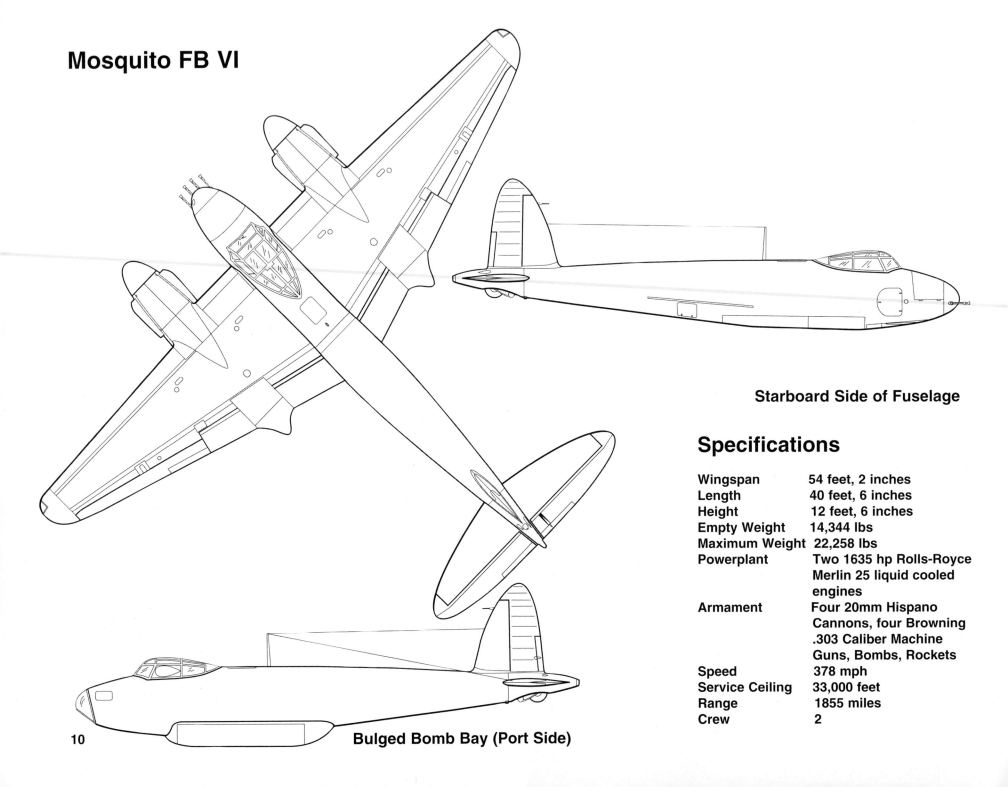

Starboard Side of Fuselage

Bulged Bomb Bay (Port Side)

Specifications

Wingspan	54 feet, 2 inches
Length	40 feet, 6 inches
Height	12 feet, 6 inches
Empty Weight	14,344 lbs
Maximum Weight	22,258 lbs
Powerplant	Two 1635 hp Rolls-Royce Merlin 25 liquid cooled engines
Armament	Four 20mm Hispano Cannons, four Browning .303 Caliber Machine Guns, Bombs, Rockets
Speed	378 mph
Service Ceiling	33,000 feet
Range	1855 miles
Crew	2

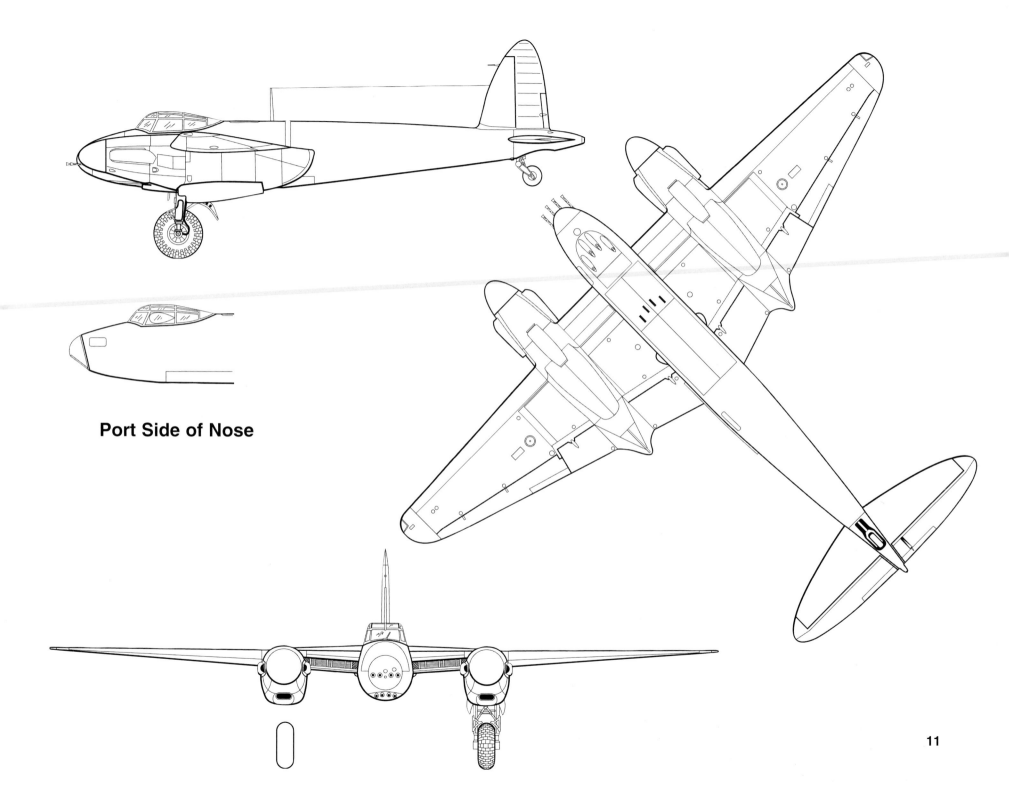

Port Side of Nose

11

(Below) The distinctive landing gear doors were mounted on two elbow-shaped hinges which allowed them to stand away from the nacelle. A removable oval panel was placed onto the door to allow inspection of the landing gear retraction pulley system.

(Above) The Mosquito Air Museum at Salisbury Hall also possesses a Mosquito Mk 35. Although the aircraft was originally equipped for PR duties, it carries markings for a B Mk 35 operating with No. 571 (Pathfinder Force) Squadron in 1944/45.

Mosquito Main Landing Gear

(Above and Below) A single hydraulic jack attached to the right radius rod retracted the landing gear. The radius rod pulled on the elbow joint in the right radius rod which collapsed the rod and pulled the compression struts back and up. Transverse rods carried the load from the right strut to the left strut.

Mosquito wheel brakes were pneumatically operated by a compressor driven by the port engine. Operating air was fed from the compressor via a pipe attached to the rear of the compression strut. Maximum pressure was approximately 100 pounds per square inch. The solid wheel hub holding two brakes was the most common style used on the Mosquito. Early variants used a spoked outer hub with a single brake.

The front struts used a cable and roller system to extend and retract the landing gear doors. When the gear struts retracted aft and up, the wire pulled the landing gear doors closed behind them.

The retractable tail wheel used a similar shock absorbing design to that of the main landing gear. The fully castoring and self-centering wheel was mounted between a pivoting cantilever fork.

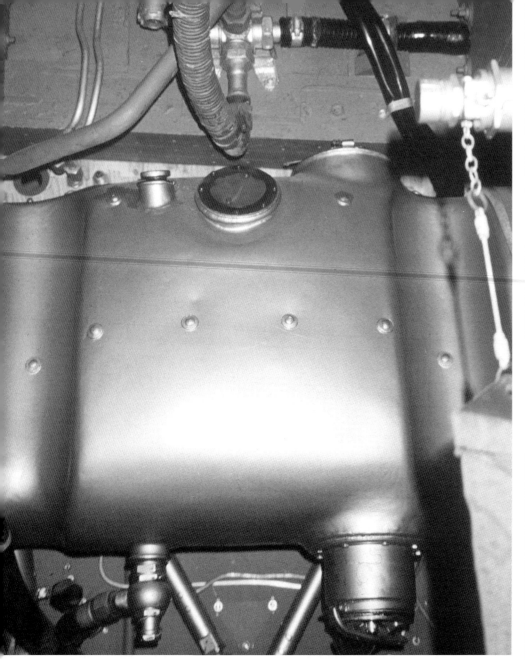

Non-self sealing oil tanks were mounted on the rear face of the forward wheel well bulkhead. The tanks had a 15.75 gallon capacity and were filled via the capped oil filler port on the side of the tank. A dipstick used to check the oil level was located to the left of the cap. The tanks featured a rapid warming chamber and a reserve supply for feathering the propellers.

14

A tow bar could be fitted to the lugs at the end of the tail wheel fork. The towing arm could be pivoted up to 45 degrees left or right. The tail wheel was retractable, but not enclosed by doors. A small part of the tire remained visible below the fuselage.

A removable fairing under the horizontal stabilizers provided access to the tail wheel bay. Three front and two rear quarter turn fasteners held the fairing panel in place. The fasteners were held in place by metal strips riveted to the panel. A wing fuel drop tank is upside down behind the tail wheel.

Early Mosquitos were fitted with standard tail wheel tires. Most, if not all, later Mosquitos were fitted with these special Dunlop anti-shimmy tires with the larger diameter outer edges. The edges prevented the wheel from excessive wobbling during taxi, take off, and landing.

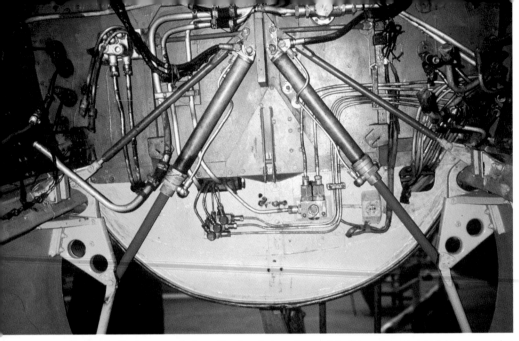

Hydraulic jacks mounted on the bomb bay forward bulkhead were used to retract the bomb bay doors. The hydraulic jack rams are fitted with a red sleeve.

The bomb bay fuel tanks were self sealing with red Linatex fabric. Both tanks were joined with a pair of crossfeed pipes. Tail surface control cables ran along the port wall of the bomb bay.

Parallel longitudinal beams mounted in the bomb bay roof separated the bomb bay fuel tanks and strengthened the fuselage structure. The bay fuel tanks fitted into the semi-circular fittings in the roof and were held in place with the straps hanging from the sides.

The aft edges of the bomb bay doors are fitted with the additional support arms. The interior of the bomb bay and doors was normally painted grey-green. Bomber variants could carry up to four 500 pound bombs in the bomb bay, while PR variants carried a variety of aerial cameras.

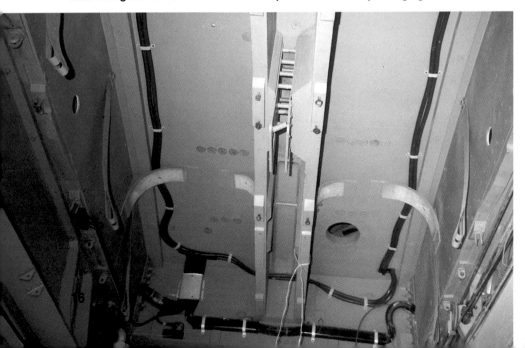

The aft fuselage and fixed tail surfaces were skinned with plywood and were relatively featureless except for stiffeners and access panels. The rudder and elevator were originally fabric covered, but later Mosquitos had the elevators skinned with metal.

The fuselage aft of the tail wheel mounting bulkhead is covered with a multi-piece tail cone. The removable lower sections provide access to the tail wheel bay. The tail cone could contain one or two white navigation lights depending on the variant.

The gap between the vertical fin and fuselage was covered with a formed metal fairing held in place by six screws on each side. The circular metal plate covers access to the fin front spar attachment lugs.

The port horizontal stabilizer had an antenna wire attachment lug set into the leading edge with a patch of doped fabric.

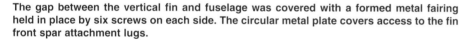

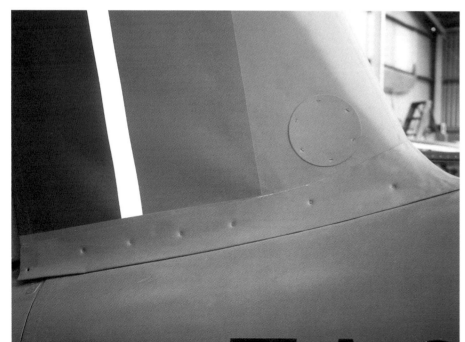

Trim tabs were set into the inner trailing edge of each elevator. The tab actuating rods were covered with a metal fairing. The fairing was on the upper surface of the starboard elevator and the under side of the port elevator.

The small teardrop shaped bulged cover on the left covers the elevator control arm and cables. The larger bulged cover on the right covers the elevator static balance. The semi-circular cover plate directly aft of the rudder provided access to the elevator's center hinge.

The vertical fin was constructed of spruce and plywood ribs attached to two wooden spars and skinned with plywood. The spars were then bolted to the two aftermost fuselage bulkheads. The leading edge of the fin also contained the pitot tube and an attachment lug for the radio antenna.

The rudder trim tab was located on the lower trailing edge of the rudder. The tab was actuated via a cockpit cranking lever and cables. The tab actuating rod was mounted on the port side of the rudder. A small mass balance projected forward from under the tab.

The observer's oval shaped front panel was optically flat to eliminate distortion. Two additional perspex panels were fitted into the sides of the nose. The nose compartment was extremely cramped.

The nose side windows were mounted in most of the bomber and PR variants. These aircraft also featured a pointed windscreen. A protective cover has been fitted into the radiator inlet in the inner wing leading edge. Bulged or blistered windows were common on bomber and PR Mosquitos, but less so on fighters and fighter bombers.

The Mosquito B Mk 35 featured the standard perspex nose glazing fitted to the bomber and PR variants. The small bubble above the optical flat covered a white navigation light. Some aircraft also had an inverted 'U' shaped tube above the optical flat for dispensing deicing liquid.

The exterior windscreen framing was characterized by large flat metal strips. The strips held armor glass and hinged front quarter panels.

The Mosquito canopy consisted mainly of metal tubes bolted and screwed to the fuselage. The windscreen was made from armor glass, while the remainder of the canopy was formed perspex. Bomber and PR aircraft had a pointed windscreen. An escape hatch was incorporated into the top of the canopy. Many bomber and PR Mosquitos were fitted with bulged or blistered side and top panels to improve visibility.

The emergency dinghy (raft) was located in a compartment directly behind the canopy. The dinghy contained glove type paddles, a signal pistol, emergency rations, and water.

The dinghy box was released and the dinghy inflated via an immersion switch or a manual release in the cockpit. The immersion switch functioned automatically when the aircraft was ditched.

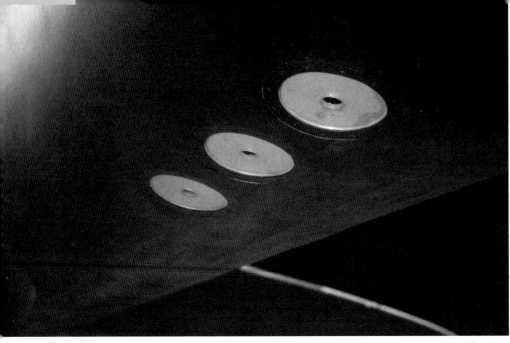

The starboard side of the lower rear fuselage housed three downward facing identification lights. The lights were tinted red, green, and amber (yellow) from front to rear and were operated individually via switches in the cockpit.

Mosquitos were originally equipped with a fixed radio mast, however, many aircraft had the mast replaced by one or two whip aerials. Both the whip aerials and fixed masts were mounted into circular fittings on the aircraft spine.

A rear fuselage access hatch was located on the starboard side of the fuselage below and behind the wing trailing edge. The hatch allowed maintenance access to electrical, hydraulic, and other components contained within the aft fuselage. An external fuselage strengthening strake ran across the top of the hatch.

Later Mosquito variants were fitted with a 'universal' wing which had all the necessary fittings for a variety of roles and equipment — drop tanks, night fighter radar aerials, and strike aircraft rocket and bomb racks. This aircraft is also fitted with a paddle bladed propeller.

The wings were primarily built of spruce and plywood ribs and stringers which were covered with plywood sheeting. All seams were filled and smoothed, leaving the surface broken only by the control surfaces and various access covers. The wing surfaces could support a load factor of 41 tons.

Teardrop-shaped wing tank fuel filler access ports were located on the upper wing surfaces on both sides of the engine nacelles. The rectangular panel covers one of four fuel tank vent pipe access holes.

The Mosquito's landing flaps ran from the wing root to the aileron, but were split by the extended engine nacelle. The aft section of the nacelle housed the flap actuator and a torque tube linking the inner and outer flap sections. The flaps were constructed using wooden ribs skinned with plywood.

The flaps could be lowered from zero degrees to a maximum of 45° as well as any intermediate position. The flaps were set to zero degrees for taxiing, 15°-25° for takeoff, and 45° for landing. The flaps were usually up when the aircraft was parked since retracting the flaps was part of the pilot's shut down checklist..

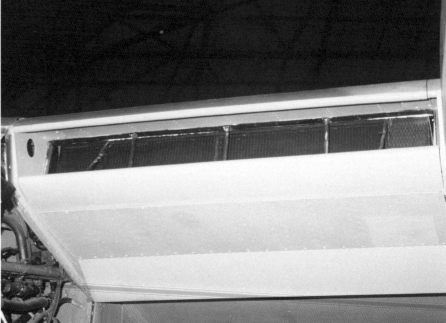

Each engine had a radiator mounted in the leading edge of the inner wing section. The radiator was flanked by an oil cooler on the outside and a cabin heater core on the inside. The air flow was controlled via the moveable flap on the under wing surface behind the radiator.

Wing Radiator, Oil Cooler, and Cabin Heater
(Starboard Wing Shown)

Later variants of the Mosquito — such as this B Mk 35 — were fitted with uprated Merlin engines equipped with a two-stage supercharger. These engines required a revised cowling with an intercooler scoop located below the propeller spinner and an elongated carburetor air scoop. The cowl panels were metal and removable for maintenance.

The Mosquito B 35 was powered by two 12 cylinder, 1710 horsepower, Rolls-Royce Merlin 114 supercharged engines. The engines provided the aircraft with a top speed of 415 mph at 42,000 feet. This is the starboard side of the number two (starboard) engine.

The port side of the same engine above reveals the large diameter coolant pipe leading from the coolant header tank at left down to the engine driven coolant circulating pump beneath the rear of the engine. The magneto cooling pipe is sandwiched between the rear exhaust stub and the radiator.

The coolant pipe leading from the header tank to the pump is fastened to the lower engine bearer with two clips. The silver unit beneath the engine is the hydraulic pump.

Merlin engines with two-stage superchargers had an extra air scoop located under the spinner. The scoop fed air into the supercharger intercooler. Behind the scoop is the intercooler's louvered outlet port. Below the intercooler outlet is the carburetor air scoop. An ice guard is fitted over the mouth of the scoop, but these were not always fitted.

Two removable panels provided access to the flap actuator and the torque tube linking the inner and outer flap sections. The spanwise raised strip in front of the flap access panel covers the rear wing spar.

The fuel tanks on either side of the engine nacelles were covered by removable access panels under the wing. These panels formed part of the wing's stressed skin. Each wing was equipped with a flip down landing light.

Many later Mosquito variants had an additional pair of landing/taxi lights mounted in the starboard wing leading edge and covered by a single piece of curved perspex. These are also believed to have been used as an identification light to friendly aircraft.

A small formation light was mounted on the inner wing tip trailing edge. Light was emitted through small slots and was only visible from behind the aircraft.

The leading edge of each wing tip was fitted with a clear perspex cover. Inside the cover was a colored navigation light — red to port and blue-green to starboard. The colored bulbs were accessed via the rectangular cover immediately adjacent to the clear cover. Some Mosquito variants had a second pair of lights mounted in the wing tip trailing edge.

Both all-metal ailerons were equipped with a trim tab set into the inner trailing edge. The port aileron trim tab also served as a balance tab.

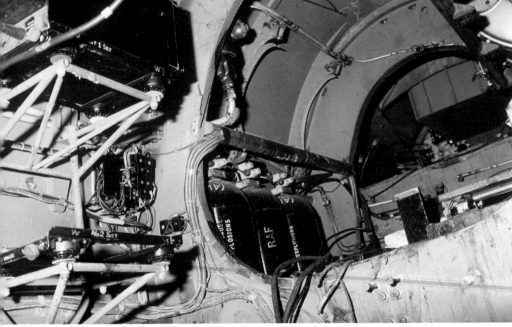

Looking forward from the starboard aft fuselage hatch reveals the radio mounting trays on the port side of the fuselage behind the number four bulkhead. Further forward are the compressed air cylinders. The interior fuselage was painted overall interior grey-green.

Mosquito bomber and PR variants were equipped with a downward hinging crew access door under the starboard side of the nose. The door could be jettisoned in flight by depressing the pedal at the top. The circular viewport allowed the use of a drift sight for navigation purposes.

Looking up through the entry hatch reveals the tubular metal structure of the canopy. Mosquito canopies were equipped with a variety of flat, bulged, and/or blistered side panels. Many PR variants were also equipped with a blistered panel in the upper escape hatch. The oval panel is a 'knock-in' plug to allow outside rescuers access to the yellow hatch release lever. The hatch release was normally painted red. The black knurled wheel operated an air vent.

A silver hydraulic reservoir tank was mounted opposite the compressed air cylinders on the starboard side. Forward is the number three bulkhead and the rear wing spar. The dinghy box is hanging down from the top of the fuselage above the wing spar.

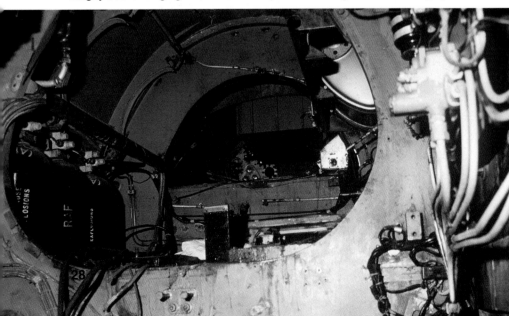

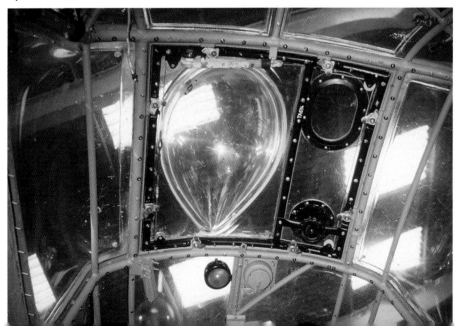

The main instrument panel was located on the port side of the cockpit and contained all of the primary flying, navigation, and engine instruments. The red knobbed lever at right operated the landing gear. The levers to its left and right respectively operate the bomb bay doors and flaps. The compass binnacle is at lower left.

A subpanel is located above the passageway to the nose compartment immediately to the right of the main instrument panel . The subpanel contains the two propeller feathering buttons, electrical switches, and a drift meter for a ground position radio. The instrument and electrical panels were generally painted black.

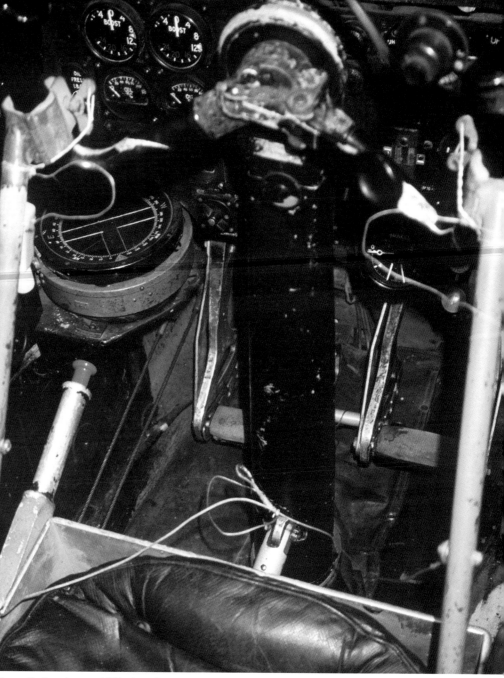

Mosquito bomber and PR aircraft were equipped with a control column and wheel. The elevator control rod was attached to the base of the column. Two rods clipped to the seat locked the control column. The silver handle on the seat pan adjusts the seat's height.

The windscreen framing served as a mount for the rudder trim knob on bomber and PR Mosquitos. The control cables extended downward through the instrument panel.

The engine control quadrant was mounted on the port cockpit sidewall and contained the throttles and propeller controls. The compass binnacle is directly in front of the throttle quadrant. Directly above the throttles is the elevator trim indicator dial. The cockpit sidewall is painted grey-green, while the throttle quadrant and other equipment are black.

The left front windscreen quarter panel was hinged at the rear and swung back into the cockpit. This type of window was fitted to bomber and PR aircraft with pressurized cockpits. Non-pressurized aircraft used a sliding window.

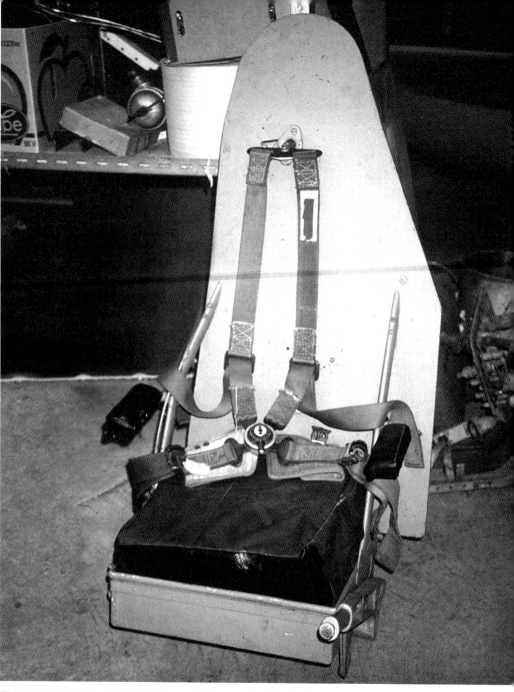

The pilot's seat consisted of a formed metal seat pan attached to an armored back plate. The shoulder harness was attached to a ring which was secured to the top of the back plate.

The seat was equipped with folding padded armrests. The back plate was asymmetrical to conform to the interior fuselage sides.

(Above) This Mosquito fighter at the Yorkshire Air Museum in England is a combination of parts from several Marks, but is being rebuilt to represent a Mosquito NF II Night Fighter — the first night fighter variant to see operational service.

(Below) The aircraft is complete except for bomb doors and the wing area between the fuselage and the engine nacelles. This Mosquito is also equipped with the needle-style propeller blades common to all early Mosquito variants.

The Airborne Interception (AI) Mk IV radar equipment used an arrow shaped transmitter antenna mounted in the extreme nose of the aircraft, while the receiver antennas were mounted above and below the wing tips. Four .303 caliber machine gun barrels protruded through the holes below the radar antenna.

The gun bay was covered by a pair of removable hatches split port and starboard. The inner surfaces of the gun bay were painted grey-green (FS 34226).

The inside of the nose cone contained integral fairings for the machine gun barrels and a rack for a G42 or G45 gun camera. The gun camera looked out an aperture above and between the two left most machine guns.

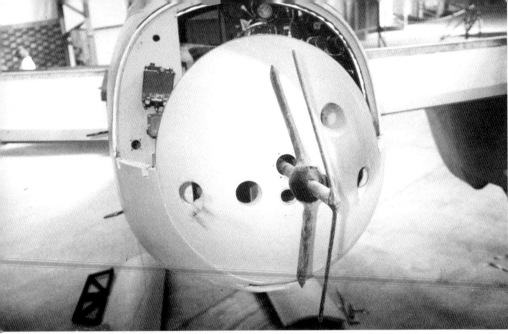

The gun camera looked through the aperture in the upper port side of the nose cone. The rectangular black box on the gun bay bulkhead is the windscreen wiper motor. The rear of the gun bay was usually covered with armor plate. The armor plate, along with the armored windscreen, were designed to prevent return fire from German bombers from entering the crew compartment.

The machine gun bay was covered by two panels split longitudinally. The panels were held together along their centerline by two 'J' hooks on the port panel which fit into brackets on the starboard panel. The inner surfaces of the gun bay panels were painted grey-green.

All Mosquito fighter and fighter-bomber variants were fitted with a single piece flat windscreen made from bullet proof glass. A steel bullet deflector strip ran along the base of the windscreen. The open rectangular bracket at the base of the windscreen housed a single windscreen wiper blade.

The Mosquito fighter canopy structure was generally identical to that of the bomber variants apart from the flat windscreen. The welded tube frames were covered with perspex and bolted and screwed to the fuselage. The perspex side panels on fighters were usually flat.

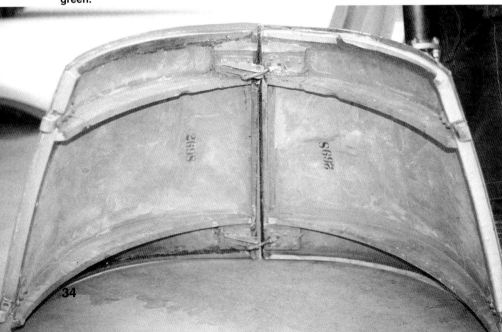

The Spirit of Val

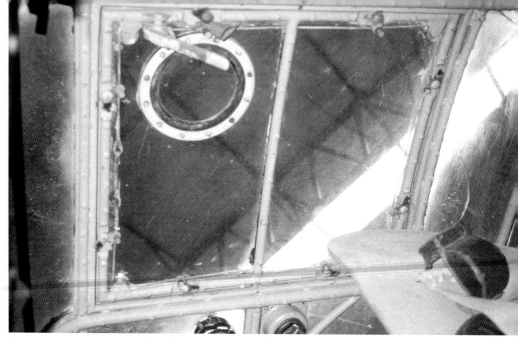

The tubular canopy frame was covered by formed perspex. A single flat framing strip ran along the center line up to the upper escape hatch. Additional flat strips were added to the sides and the windscreen. A signal flare port was located on the port side of the framing strip just behind the hatch.

An escape hatch is centered in the upper section of the canopy. The handle at upper left released the catches around the periphery of the hatch. The handle was normally painted red while the interior canopy structure was painted grey-green.

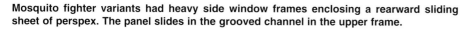

Mosquito fighter variants had heavy side window frames enclosing a rearward sliding sheet of perspex. The panel slides in the grooved channel in the upper frame.

A signal gun socket was mounted in the canopy behind the pilot's seat. The cockpit roof lamp was next to the signal port. The entire canopy structure was built as a unit and added to the wooden fuselage shells during the final assembly process.

35

The pilot's seat was secured in place by two brackets mounted on the ledge behind the seat. The small handle on the corner of the seat pan was used to release the shoulder harness via the black cable snaking up the starboard side of the seat. The two V-shaped rods secure the control stick.

The center of the main instrument panel housed the primary flying instruments at the top, followed by the landing gear and flap position indicators, the red landing gear selector, a pair of oxygen indicators, and a single brake hydraulic pressure indicator.

Bomber Control Column

Fighter Control Stick

Rudder Pedals

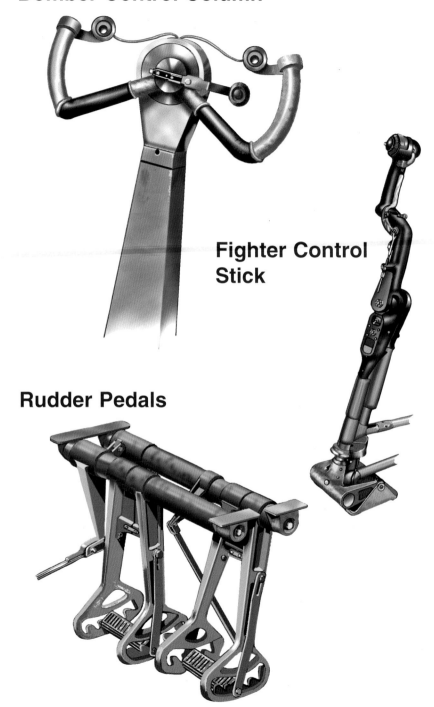

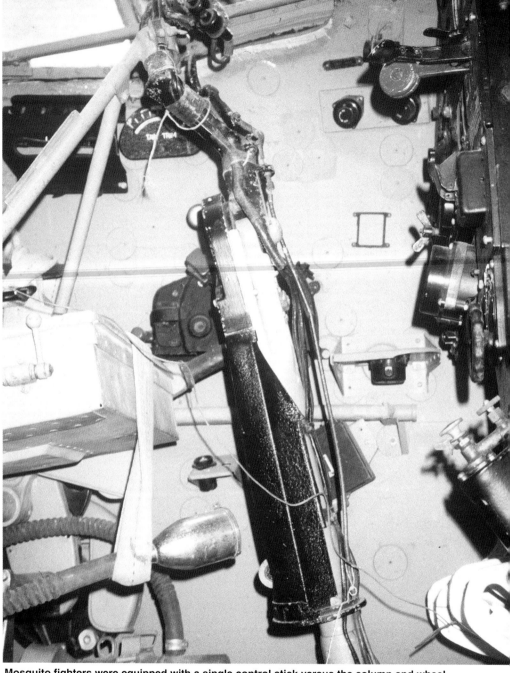

Mosquito fighters were equipped with a single control stick versus the column and wheel of the bomber and PR variants. The entire stick moved forward and backward, but only the upper half moved from side to side for aileron control — an arrangement similar to that of the single-engine Supermarine Spitfire and Hawker Hurricane fighters.

Additional instruments and controls were mounted on the starboard sidewall above the crew entry hatch. The box contained fuel gauges, ID light switches, the IFF detonator switches — linked with a strip across their top — and red engine fire extinguisher buttons. Just above the box is the lower track for the sliding front quarter window.

The lower right portion of the box contained the fuel gauges for the inner, center, and outer fuel tanks. The bottom row consists of the windscreen wiper control, an air temperature gauge, and a clock.

The throttle quadrant is mounted on the cockpit's port sidewall. The two round knobs are the throttles. The two square knobs are the propeller controls. The small lever at the rear of the quadrant controls the fuel mixture. The quadrant is black, while all of the knobs are red-orange.

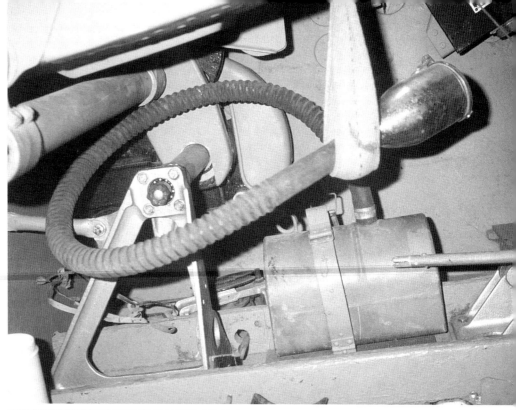

(Above) The fuel control panel was mounted on the bulkhead behind the pilot and to the left of the navigator's seat. The silver fuel cocks allowed the engines to feed from various fuel tanks. The OUTER tanks were used for engine startup, taxi, and flight, while the MAIN SUPPLY tanks used fuel from the inner and center wing tanks. The yellow buttons at the top of the panel were the engine cut outs.

(Above Right) Mosquito flights, especially those of the photo-reconnaissance (PR) aircraft, could be long. The pilot was provided with a relief system mounted under his seat. The system consisted of a funnel, a corrugated flexible tube, and a sanitary tank.

(Right) A fuel gallery was located on the starboard side of the bomb bay. The system provided pressure refueling for the inner tanks, constant fuel pressure to the engines, and a low fuel pressure warning to the pilot.

Looking forward through the hatch reveals the numbers four and three bulkheads, the wing box center section, the base of the antenna mast attached to the wing box, and the lower half of the dinghy box.

The antenna mast is channeled through a circular plate in the top of the fuselage. The dinghy hatch was located in front of the antenna mast. The small cover plate in the dinghy hatch lid permitted inspection of the dinghy's CO_2 inflation bottle.

Looking back through the starboard side aft fuselage hatch reveals the rudder cables and pulleys, electrical lines, and black cover over the tail wheel strut. The interior of the wooden fuselage was painted grey-green.

Lugs at the base of the vertical fin's front and rear spars were attached to the top of the number six and seven fuselage bulkheads. The base of the vertical fin was covered with a metal fairing.

The metal rudder trim tab was fitted with a small mass balance projecting forward under the rudder.

The light alloy rudder frame is entirely skinned with metal. The actuating rod for the metal trim tab was located on the port side of the rudder. Early Mosquitos had fabric covered elevators and rudder, but these were replaced by metal skins when high diving speeds began ripping the fabric off the frames.

Mosquito Night Fighter Variants

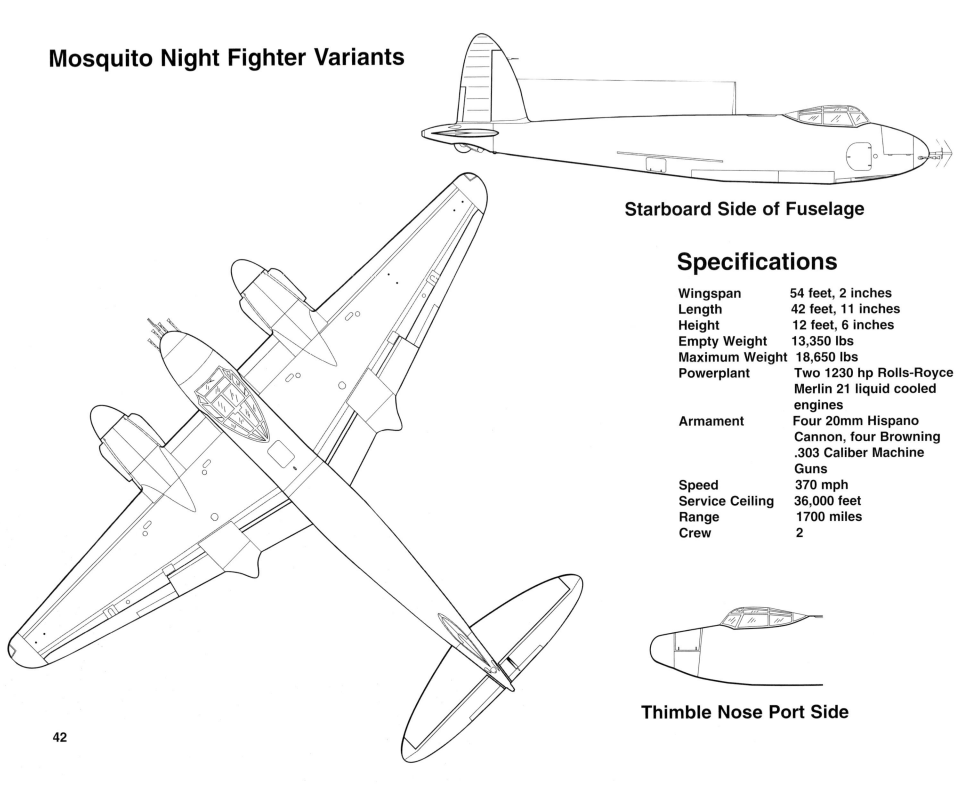

Starboard Side of Fuselage

Specifications

Wingspan	54 feet, 2 inches
Length	42 feet, 11 inches
Height	12 feet, 6 inches
Empty Weight	13,350 lbs
Maximum Weight	18,650 lbs
Powerplant	Two 1230 hp Rolls-Royce Merlin 21 liquid cooled engines
Armament	Four 20mm Hispano Cannon, four Browning .303 Caliber Machine Guns
Speed	370 mph
Service Ceiling	36,000 feet
Range	1700 miles
Crew	2

Thimble Nose Port Side

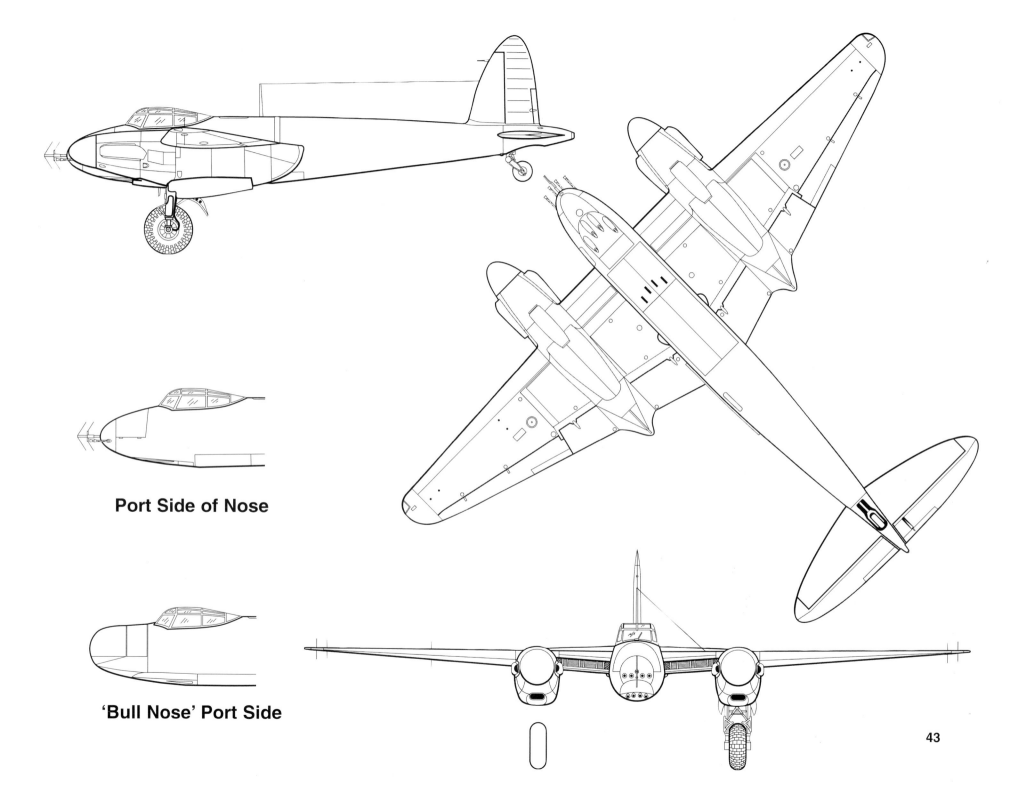

Port Side of Nose

'Bull Nose' Port Side

43

The leading edge of the vertical fin incorporated the heated pitot tube at the top and an attachment lug for a wire aerial. Activation of the pitot heat discolored the end of the pitot tube.

Removal of the tail cone sections reveals the horizontal stabilizer spars, the elevator torque tube, and its bellcrank. The horizontal stabilizer was of all wood construction.

The elevator trim tab actuating jack was bolted to the back of the rear stabilizer spar. The elevators were originally metal framed and covered with fabric. Metal skinned elevators were introduced in 1943. The rudder control rod is attached to the rudder control arm at the base of the rudder.

Some Mosquitos carried two lights on the tail cone. The upper light is the standard white navigation light. The lower light is a formation light. This Mosquito is equipped with metal skinned elevators.

The forward gun bay housed four .303 caliber machine guns, four ammunition boxes, and four feed chutes. The boxes held up to 1000 rounds. The rounds were fed through the feed chutes to prevent jamming. Empty cases were ejected via chutes into a container below the guns. A recoil spring is barely visible on the weapon in the foreground just in front of the gun breech. The machine gun bay and ammunition boxes were painted grey-green.

All four Browning .303 caliber machine guns were fitted with conical flash suppressors. The machine guns fired at a rate of approximately 1000 rounds per minute. The circular opening at the lower right permitted access to the spent cartridge case compartment below the guns.

The guns were staggered horizontally to provide clearance for the feed and ejection chutes. All but one of the guns has had the conical flash suppressor removed. The middle pair of guns are mounted in trunnions attached to the support tube running between the port and starboard side.

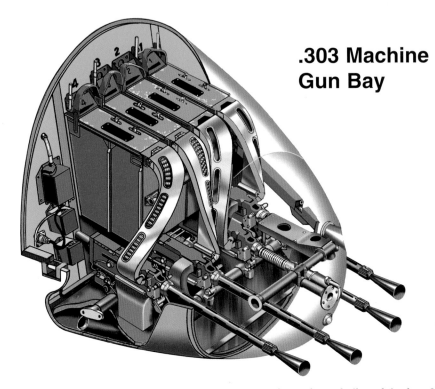

.303 Machine Gun Bay

The Mosquito Mk XVIII was modified to carry a six-pounder (57mm) gun in lieu of the four 20mm Hispano cannons. The gun and mount weighed almost 1600 lbs and was offset to starboard and angled slightly downward. The cannon armed Mosquitos — known as the 'Tse-Tse' for an African fly which spreads sleeping sickness — were used as gunships and were particularly effective against shipping.

The lower fuselage gun bay housed four 20mm Hispano cannons. The guns were staggered to provide clearance for the feed chutes. Each gun was fed from ammunition boxes containing up to 225 rounds per gun. The gun bay took up the forward half of the bomb bay and restricted the internal bomb load to two 500 lb bombs.

The six pounder gun held 25 rounds in a rack mounted to starboard. Four of the rounds are visible in the rack. Mosquitos equipped with the 57mm gun did not carry the four 20mm fuselage cannons and usually dispensed with two of the four Browning .303 caliber machine guns in the nose. The remaining pair of machine guns were used for sighting purposes.

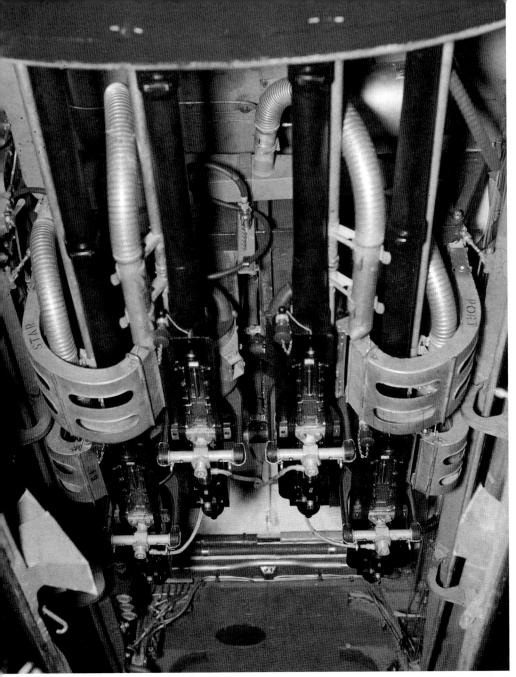

The 20mm cannons in the lower fuselage bay were staggered vertically and fore-and-aft to provide clearance for the mounts and ammunition feed chutes. The corrugated pipe channeled warm air to each cannon. A fifth tube ran forward to heat the nose mounted machine guns. The spent cartridge cases and links were ejected out the bottom of the aircraft.

The 20mm cannons were mounted in trunnions suspended from a transverse mounting beam. The guns could be adjusted laterally and vertically using the small knobs on the trunnions. The air manifold on the transverse beam and the braided lines are part of the pneumatic gun charging system.

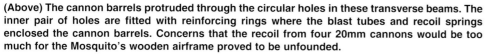

(Above) The cannon barrels protruded through the circular holes in these transverse beams. The inner pair of holes are fitted with reinforcing rings where the blast tubes and recoil springs enclosed the cannon barrels. Concerns that the recoil from four 20mm cannons would be too much for the Mosquito's wooden airframe proved to be unfounded.

(Above Right) The reinforcing rings for the outer pair of guns are located on the lower section of the number four bulkhead. The interior of the lower gun bay was painted overall grey-green. The four Hispano cannons carried by night fighters and fighter bombers occupies the forward half of the bomb bay. Night fighters usually carried extra fuel in the remaining space, but fighter bombers were still capable of carrying a pair of 500 lb bombs in addition to their underwing armament of rockets or bombs.

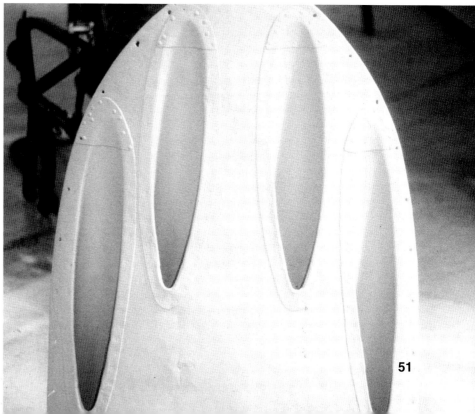

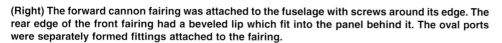

(Right) The forward cannon fairing was attached to the fuselage with screws around its edge. The rear edge of the front fairing had a beveled lip which fit into the panel behind it. The oval ports were separately formed fittings attached to the fairing.

The left main gear of the Yorkshire Air Museum's Mosquito displays the typical square tread tire pattern used by most Mosquitos during WW II, although some Mosquitos were fitted with smooth or circumferential treaded tires. The wheel on this aircraft has been fitted backwards — the brake line fitting in front of the axle should be facing aft.

The front fender guards are attached to the outside of the main gear struts. These are of simpler construction than those found on bomber and PR Mosquitos. The curved plate behind the wheel is a mud guard.

The lower section of the X-braces are attached to the front and rear of the compression legs. The upper section is only linked to the rear of the legs. The gear door retraction cables are fed through the holes in the horizontal brace just below the center of the X-brace.

The upper end of the retraction jack attaches to the wheel well side wall. A hydraulic fitting to operate the jack is incorporated into the lower end of the jack housing.

The hollow steel radius rods are attached to brackets on the lower edge of the rear wing spar.

The upper ends of the compression struts are attached to a transverse rod which is attached and braced to the front wing spar. The lower section of this bracing also serves as the lower mounting point for the engine bearers. The cross bracing and attachment points are normally hidden behind an oil tank mounted on the bulkhead. The bulkhead functions as a firewall separating the engine compartment from the wheel well.

The lower end of the retraction jack attaches to an elbow joint on the right radius rod. This section also incorporates the latch which holds the gear in the up position.

Mosquitos were routinely fitted with mudguards. These guards were mounted on a pair of flanges secured to a transverse beam attached to the lower radius rods. The inner mounting flange was located further inward than the outer flange.

Mosquitos used three bladed De Havilland Hydromatic propellers. This propeller has the early style 'needle' blades. Later variants used a wider paddle blade. The propellers were fully feathering. The blades were normally painted black with yellow warning tips.

Mosquito engines were fitted with a wide variety of exhaust manifolds during their wartime service. The engine of this fighter variant has the six exhaust ports on the port side ganged into two fishtail style outlets — a design often referred to as a 'saxophone' exhaust. The entire unit is shrouded on the inside to prevent hot exhaust gases from seeping into the engine bay. An external flame dampening shroud was also fitted. The silver glycol header tank is visible just behind the spinner.

The Yorkshire Air Museum's Mosquito is fitted with a pair of Rolls-Royce Merlin 21/23 engines. The engines are equipped with the two outlet style known as the 'saxophone' pattern. The copper colored pipes are part of the coolant system. All of the cowl panels were removable for maintenance access.

The removal of the side and top cowl panels reveals the rocker arm covers, exhaust manifold, engine bearers, and the supercharger housing of the Merlin engine. The glycol header tank has been removed from its location behind the spinner.

(Above) The fishtail outlets on the 'saxophone' pattern exhaust created a jet effect for the exhaust which marginally increased the aircraft's speed. The exhaust manifold has prominent weld beads.

Engine Colors

The overall color of the engine block, supercharger and reduction gear housings, and oil sump are semi-gloss black or light gray. The cylinder heads and rocker covers were usually semi-gloss black. The firewall, engine bearers, and interior cowl panels are grey-green. The interiors of the exhaust shrouds, if used, were also painted grey-green. The shroud interior was quickly discolored by heat from the exhausts. Fuel, oil, and electrical lines range from black to an aluminum color. Engine coolant pipes are characterized by a rusty copper-brown color. The exhausts are painted black, but would have a burnt metal appearance when in regular use.

(Left) The glycol header tank normally rests against the concave inner shroud behind the spinner. A silver colored vacuum pump is mounted below the tank. Suction and pressure lines run from the top and bottom of the pump respectively. Each engine powered a small vacuum pump. The pump on this starboard engine also served to pressurize the fuel tanks.

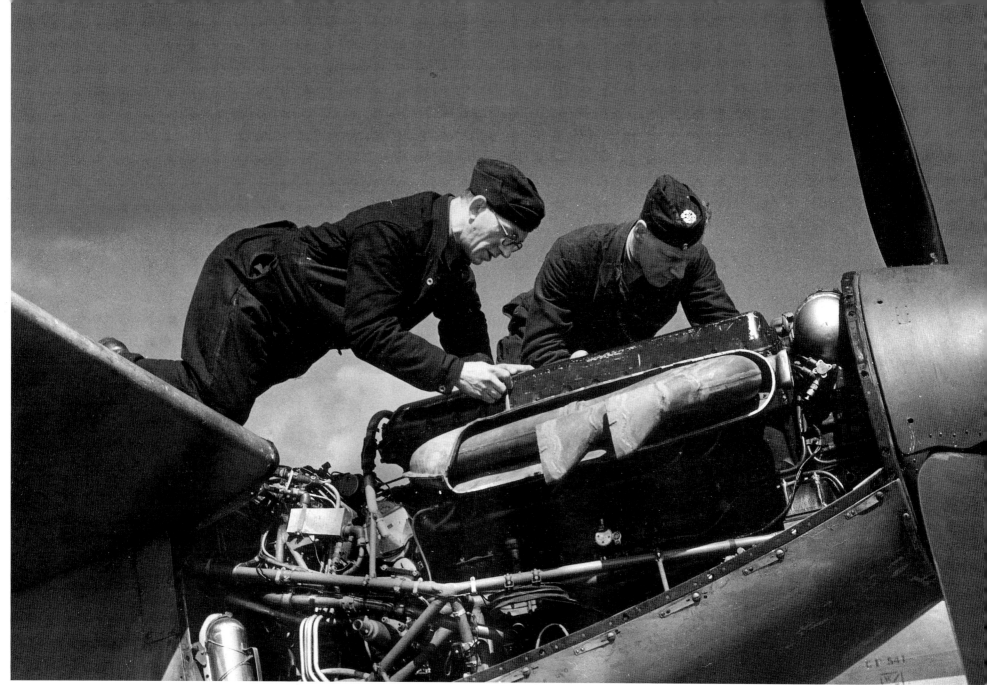

This Merlin engine has the silver glycol header tank mounted behind the spinner. The internal exhaust shrouds are also attached. Buried under the mass of wires and pipes behind the engine block is the fuel injection system and the supercharger. A small fire extinguisher bottle is mounted on the firewall.

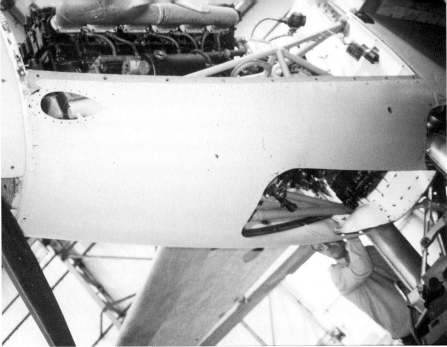

The underside of the engine was covered with a single piece cowl panel. The oblong cutout is for the carburetor air intake shroud. The teardrop cutout provided clearance for a coolant pipe. It was normally covered with a teardrop shaped blister.

The engine bearers were formed from tubular steel and attached to the front wing spar and fixed upper portion of the landing gear support structure. An engine driven generator is mounted on the block just below the second exhaust outlet. The hydraulic pump hangs down from the center of engine block.

The curved end of the large coolant pipe is routed into the coolant circulating pump. The hydraulic pump is mounted in the center of the lower engine block. The pump supplied hydraulic pressure for the landing gear and flaps. Each engine was equipped with a pump, but the loss of one meant operations at a reduced capacity.

The silver hydraulic pump is mounted below the generator. A small drain tank was mounted on the engine bearers for the fuel and hydraulic pumps, fuel vent, and supercharger. The Hydromatic oil pump is sandwiched between the tank and the coolant pipe.

Other Mosquito variants used a five exhaust stack arrangement whereby the two rearmost cylinders were ducted into a single port. A special Inconel heat resistant panel absorbed the brunt of the hot exhaust gases. The red FIRE ACCESS panel provides access to the fire extinguisher mounted on the firewall.

Directly behind the firewall at the wing joint is the aircraft jacking point. The jacking point cover has been removed. The black cylindrical object on the firewall is the boost gauge fuel trap. The bronze pipes at upper left lead to and from the wingroot mounted coolant radiator.

(Above) The wing leading edge between the tip and the engine nacelle is a separate section. The leading edges were made from spruce nose ribs reinforced with a plywood strip and covered by a preformed ply skin.

(Upper Left) The underwing stressed skins were applied diagonally to improved strength. The lower wing skins consisted of a single layer of plywood. The gray panel at lower right covers the outer wing fuel tank.

(Left) The wing tips were separate units and incorporated one or two wing tip navigation/formation lights. The center hole houses the outer azimuth aerial for the AI Mk IV radar equipment. Other aerials are mounted at the oval slot inboard from the wing tip. The aerials protrude vertically above and below the wing.

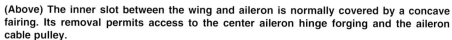

(Above) The inner slot between the wing and aileron is normally covered by a concave fairing. Its removal permits access to the center aileron hinge forging and the aileron cable pulley.

(Above Right) A bolt passing through the U-shaped hinge holds the outer portion of the aileron in place. The forged attachment is bolted to the rear wing spar. The rear wing spar also supported the aileron hinges and the landing gear radius rods.

The flap retraction jack is attached to the rear wing spar inside the aft section of the engine nacelles. The ram (not visible) is secured to a 'U' shaped arm on the flap torque tube. The torque tube passes through the back of the nacelle and links the inner and outer flap sections.

Wings and partially completed aircraft crowd the factory assembly hall. The green and grey wings in the foreground are destined for fighter and bomber aircraft, while the blue wings will be mated to PR fuselages. The wing center sections are painted interior grey-green.

(Above) A Mosquito PR Mk XVI of No. 60 Squadron, South African Air Force sits in its open dispersal in southern Italy. The airfield is one of many airfields in the Foggia complex. The red and white striped vertical fins were used as a recognition marking in the belief that the Mosquito closely resembled the Messerschmitt Me 210/410 fighter.

(Above Right) A Mosquito (RR299) sits on a ramp in October of 1970. The aircraft is camouflaged in dark green, dark sea grey, and medium sea grey normally applied to the bomber variants and bears the code letters of No. 418 (City of Edmonton) Squadron, RCAF.

(Right) Twenty-six years later, RR299 was being operated on the airshow circuit by British Aerospace until its fatal crash in July of 1996. The aircraft wore a new coat of camouflage paint and had invasion stripes added under the wings and fuselage.

Armorers fit bomb carriers to the bombs before hoisting them into the bomb bay. Bomber and fighter-bomber Mosquitos could carry up to four or two 500 pound bombs respectively in the bomb bay. The underside of the fuselage is heavily stained with soot from the four 20mm Hispano cannons. The aircraft code letter 'V' has been repeated on the nose and the camera aperture above the port machine guns has been taped over.

Another Mosquito FB Mk VI has a bomb hoisted into the bomb bay. The armorer steadies the bomb while the winch cable takes the strain of lifting it into place. The camera aperture above the port machine guns is uncovered on this aircraft. Mosquito fighter and fighter-bomber variants had the crew entry door mounted on the starboard side of the nose.

(Above) Although the Mosquito Mk XVIII had the same outline as the FB Mk VI, there was one striking difference — the Mk XVIII carried a Molins or Vickers 57mm automatic gun capable of firing up to 25 six-pounder rounds in approximately 20 seconds. The 57mm gun and its ammunition rack was mounted in lieu of the quartet of 20mm cannons in the lower fuselage. Two of the .303 caliber machine guns were usually eliminated and the remaining pair of .303s were used as a sighting aid for the 57mm gun.

(Right) Two armorers load belts of 20mm cannon rounds onto a drum reel prior to loading the belly mounted cannon. Another armorer secures the .303 caliber machine gun boxes into the nose compartment. Two additional .303 caliber ammunition containers rest in the foreground.

Mosquito Camouflage Patterns

Temperate Land Scheme

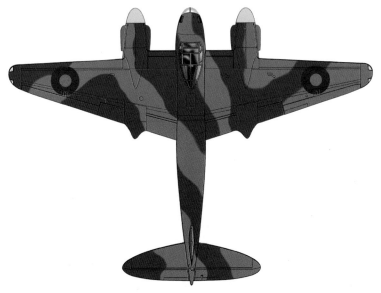

Day Fighter Scheme

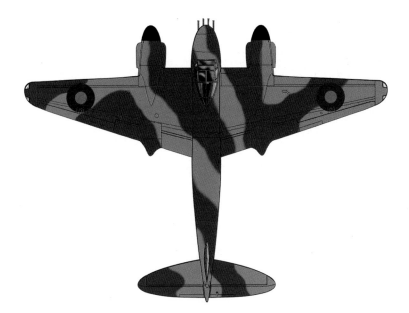

Photo Reconnaissance Scheme

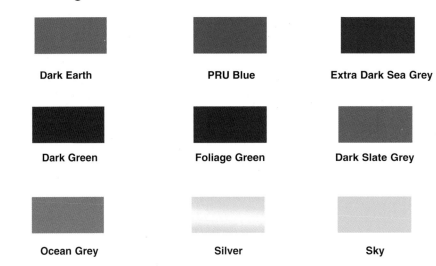

Camouflage Colors

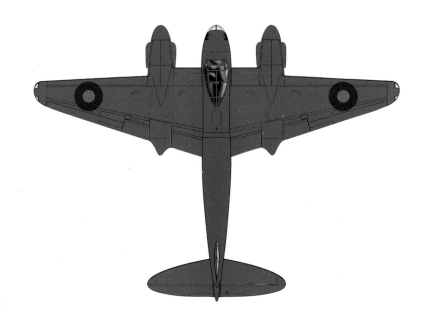

Dark Earth PRU Blue Extra Dark Sea Grey

Dark Green Foliage Green Dark Slate Grey

Ocean Grey Silver Sky

RAAF Scheme

RAAF/SEAC Scheme

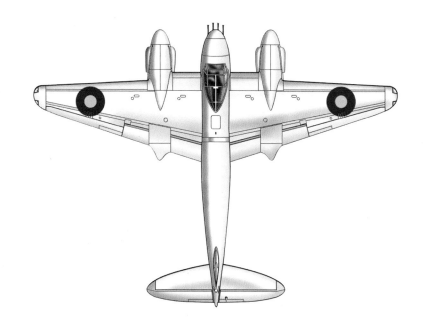

National Insignia (World War II)

RAF Type B

RAF Type C

RAF Type C.1

RAF SEAC

RAAF

USAAF

Temperate Sea Scheme

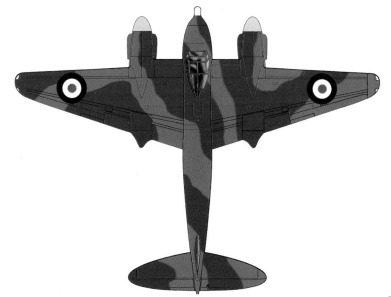

Mosquito fighter-bombers carried up to four air-to-ground rockets under each wing. The rockets could be fired in pairs or salvoed all at once. The rocket rails were slightly staggered with the outer rail being forwardmost. These are 60 lb rockets with semi-armor piercing/high explosive warheads.

A tiered rocket rail arrangement was used when the Mosquito was fitted with outer wing drop tanks. This is a test mount — rockets used operationally had four fins. The warhead is similar to the 25 lb semi-armor piercing/armor piercing shot. The rocket body was 3.25 inches in diameter and 55.25 inches long and had the solid fuel rocket motor built into the tube.

Mosquitos could carry a single drop tank under each wing. These drop tanks ranged in capacity from 50 to 100 to 200 gallons. This is a 50 gallon tank. The tanks were pressurized using the port engine vacuum pump. The rectangular slot in the center of the tank houses the mounting and support mechanism.

Wing Bomb Rack

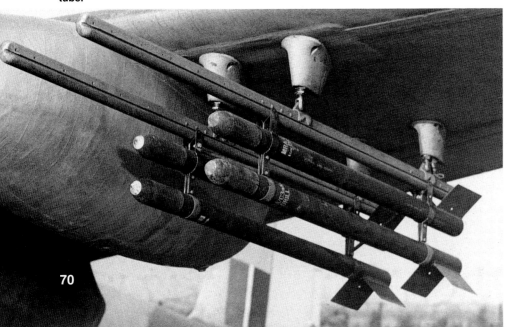

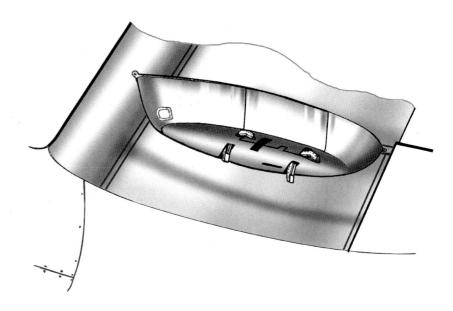

(Above) Mosquitos conducted operations on their own or in concert with other units. A pair of 105 Sqdn Mosquitos fly in formation with a No. 226 Boston light bomber during practice for a mixed force attack on the Phillips oil complex in Eindhoven, Holland. The 6 December 1942 attack was successful with the Mosquitos dropping bombs and conducting post-strike reconnaissance.

(Below) This Mosquito, believed to be an NF Mk II, was fitted with Merlin engines and nacelles from an Avro Lancaster bomber. These nacelles have large radiators under the spinners — the radiators in the inner wing leading edges have been deleted.

(Above) A flat windscreen was fitted to Mosquito fighters and fighter-bombers. This FB VI is assigned to a Polish Squadron — believed to be No. 305 Sqdn — and is being fueled prior to a sortie. Two additional air scoops are incorporated into the exhaust shrouds. The upper scoop ducts cooling air to exhaust manifold flanges, while the inner scoop directs air to the spark plugs.

71

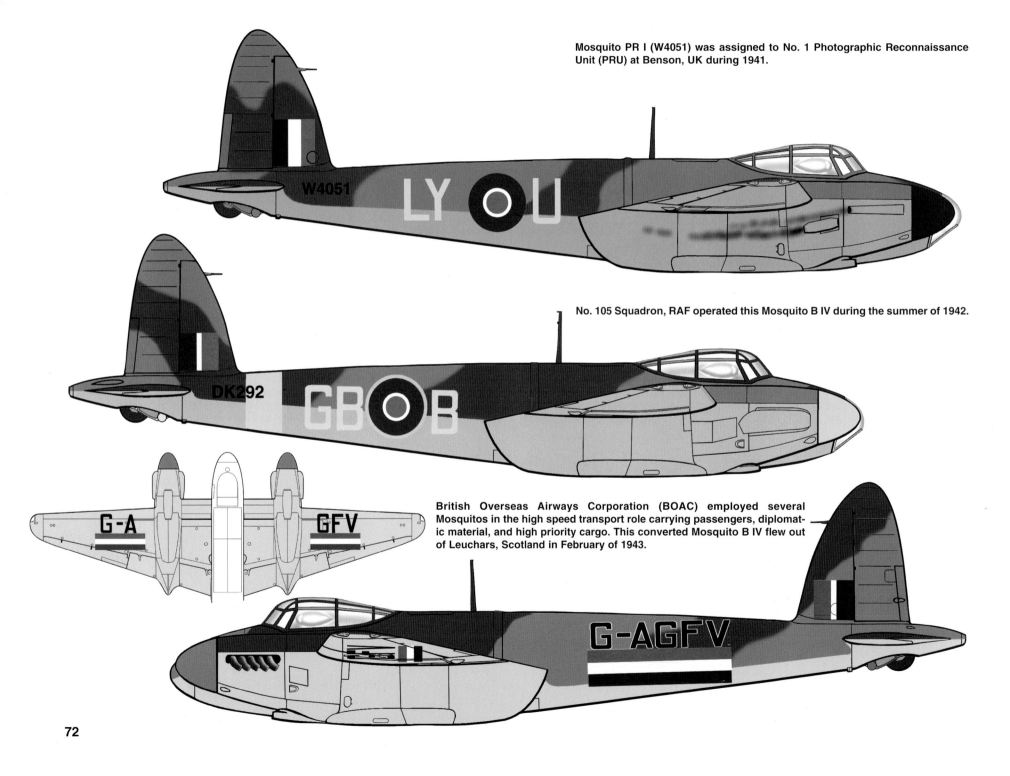

Mosquito PR I (W4051) was assigned to No. 1 Photographic Reconnaissance Unit (PRU) at Benson, UK during 1941.

No. 105 Squadron, RAF operated this Mosquito B IV during the summer of 1942.

British Overseas Airways Corporation (BOAC) employed several Mosquitos in the high speed transport role carrying passengers, diplomatic material, and high priority cargo. This converted Mosquito B IV flew out of Leuchars, Scotland in February of 1943.

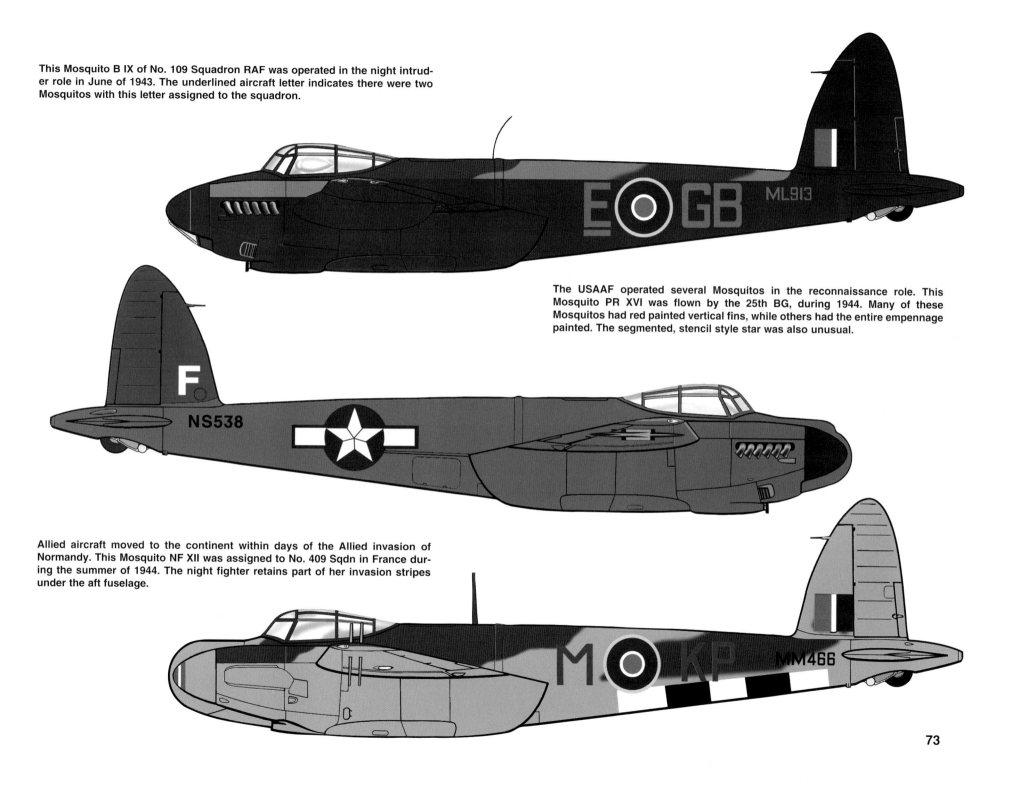

This Mosquito B IX of No. 109 Squadron RAF was operated in the night intruder role in June of 1943. The underlined aircraft letter indicates there were two Mosquitos with this letter assigned to the squadron.

The USAAF operated several Mosquitos in the reconnaissance role. This Mosquito PR XVI was flown by the 25th BG, during 1944. Many of these Mosquitos had red painted vertical fins, while others had the entire empennage painted. The segmented, stencil style star was also unusual.

Allied aircraft moved to the continent within days of the Allied invasion of Normandy. This Mosquito NF XII was assigned to No. 409 Sqdn in France during the summer of 1944. The night fighter retains part of her invasion stripes under the aft fuselage.

(Above) Several USAAF Mosquito PR Mk XVI reconnaissance aircraft were modified to carry an H2X radar in a 'bullnose' radome. This aircraft is also equipped with six downward angled fishtail exhausts and an unusual exhaust shield on the engine nacelle. The aircraft is overall Cerulean Blue with a red vertical fin. Later aircraft had the entire empennage painted red.

(Below) A Mosquito Mk XII of No. 409 (Nighthawk) Sqdn, RCAF taxies past a bombed out hangar at Carpiquet airfield, France during the summer of 1944. The aircraft has a 'bullnose' radar housing as well as barely discernible antenna rods on the wing tips. The upturned nose gives the impression of a predator sniffing the air for its prey.

(Above) A Mosquito FB VI of 464 Sqdn, RAAF taxies past the 140 Wing HQ during the summer of 1944. The black and white invasion stripes have been crudely brushed on the aft fuselage covering the squadron codes (SB) and serial number. Solid, twin brake wheel hubs were fitted to a majority of Mosquitos, although many early variants used a spoked, single braked wheel.

(Right) No. 418 Squadron, RAF received Mosquitos in May of 1943. This Mosquito (TH*X/HR155) wears a camouflage of overall Medium Sea Grey with a disruptive scheme of Dark Green sprayed onto the upper surfaces. The upper wing surfaces are stained from leaks and engine exhaust. The staining carries back to the horizontal stabilizer. The code letters were red, while the serial number was black.

The Royal Australian Air Force received a small number of Mosquitos, but did not use the type in quantity until the Australians began building their own aircraft. This Mosquito FB VI was part of the initial batch of fighter-bomber variants received from the UK.

Mosquitos were also shipped to RAF units in the China-Burma-India (CBI) theater where they were assigned to RAF Southeast Asia Command (SEAC). Dark camouflage paints were found to be detrimental to the airframe life in the heat and humidity of the CBI, consequently the RAF began painting the aircraft overall silver.

This Mosquito PR 40 was an Australian-built reconnaissance variant operated by No. 87 Sqdn RAAF at Coomalie Creek in December of 1944. The multi-color camouflage scheme such as that found on E*NA above eventually gave way to an overall Foliage Green scheme. This scheme was then supplemented by an overall silver scheme.

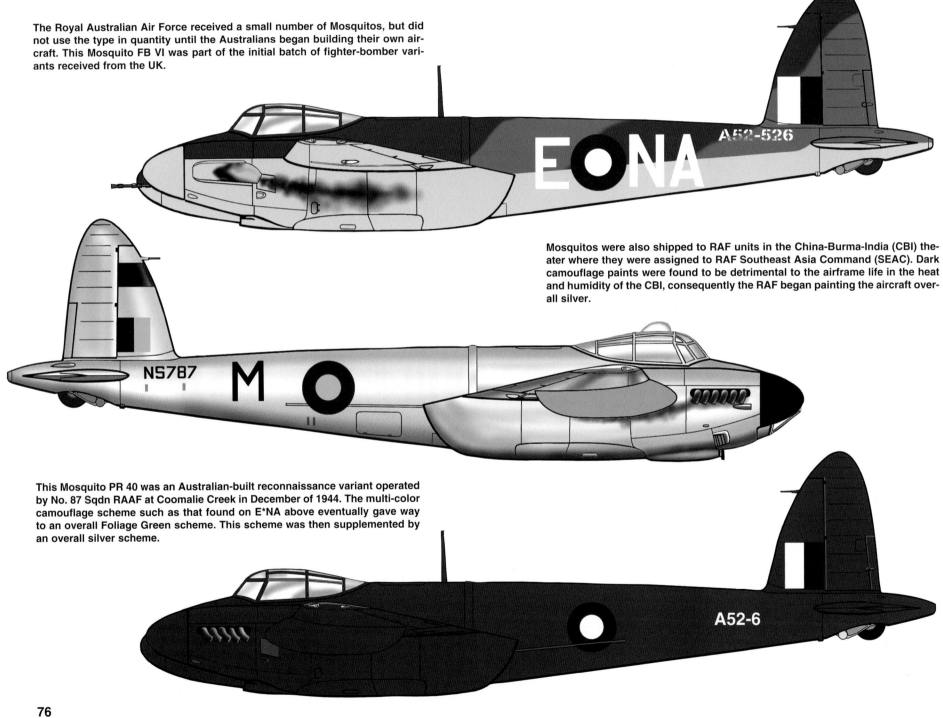

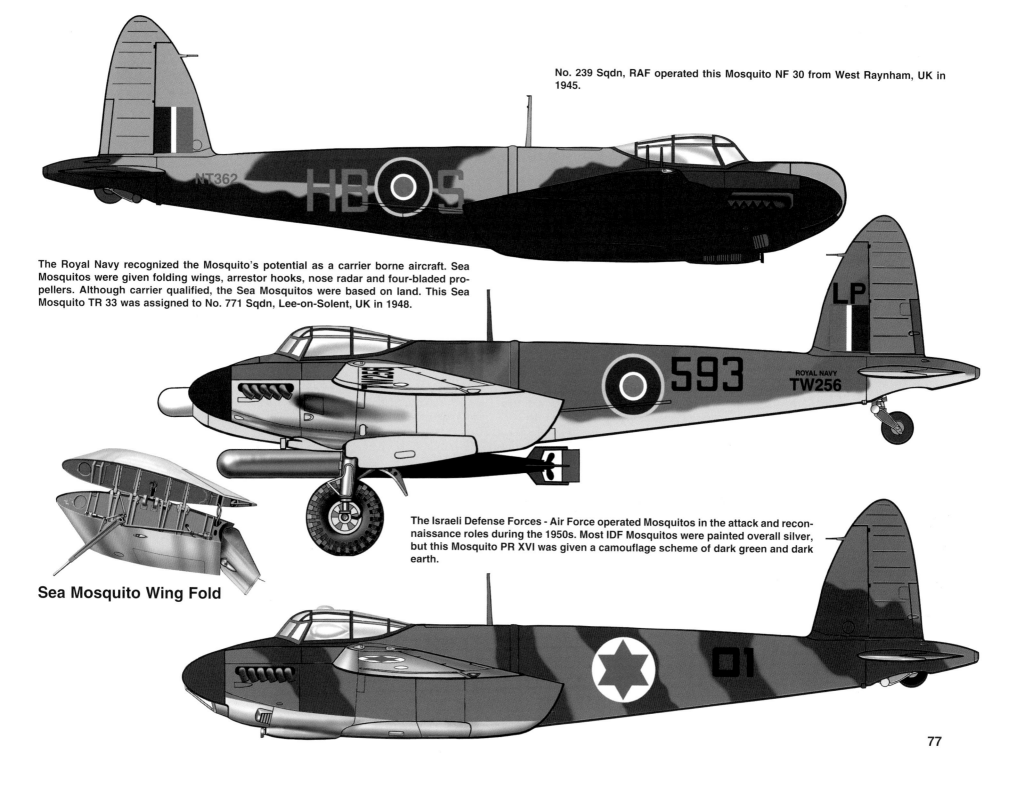

No. 239 Sqdn, RAF operated this Mosquito NF 30 from West Raynham, UK in 1945.

The Royal Navy recognized the Mosquito's potential as a carrier borne aircraft. Sea Mosquitos were given folding wings, arrestor hooks, nose radar and four-bladed propellers. Although carrier qualified, the Sea Mosquitos were based on land. This Sea Mosquito TR 33 was assigned to No. 771 Sqdn, Lee-on-Solent, UK in 1948.

Sea Mosquito Wing Fold

The Israeli Defense Forces - Air Force operated Mosquitos in the attack and reconnaissance roles during the 1950s. Most IDF Mosquitos were painted overall silver, but this Mosquito PR XVI was given a camouflage scheme of dark green and dark earth.

(Above) This Mosquito NF 36 assigned to No. 264 Sqdn was photographed shortly after WW II still wearing its wartime camouflage scheme, but also having the post-war Type D roundels and fin flash. These were similar to the early-war Type A roundels, but used brighter red and blue colors. The squadron codes (PS*J) are believed to be dark red. This aircraft also has the twin landing lights mounted in the starboard wing leading edge.

(Below) This Mosquito PR 34 acted as a navigation aircraft for De Havilland Vampire jets deploying from Egypt to Singapore in 1951. The Mosquito has been painted overall silver. During WW II silver was found to be an excellent means of protecting the wooden airframe from the effects of the tropical South Asian and Southwest Pacific climates. The scheme was widely used on RAAF and RAF South East Asia Command (SEAC) Mosquitos.

(Above) The RAF built five Mosquito NF XV high altitude fighters to counter high flying Junkers Ju 86 bombers of the Luftwaffe. The aircraft had two-stage Merlin 61 engines driving four bladed propellers, extended wing tips, reduced weight, smaller diameter wheels, and a four .303 caliber machine gun belly pack in lieu of the standard 20mm cannon armament. The aircraft never saw combat since the Luftwaffe discontinued the high-altitude bombing missions over England.

(Below) The Royal Navy received fifty production Sea Mosquito TR 33 aircraft for use in the carrier borne torpedo-bomber role. The TR 33 had single-stage Merlin engines driving four-bladed propellers, folding wings, and a tail hook in addition to a nose mounted radar and four 20mm cannons. The aircraft also had round section Lockheed oleo landing gear struts which were more suitable for carrier landings. In any event, the Sea Mosquito operated from land bases and rarely saw service on board British carriers.

Detail and Scale Series

Each book contains 72 to 80 pages of black and white and color photographs detailing the subject from prototype to final production variant inside and out. Eighty page books include additional color and profile paintings. All include scale drawings.

8248 SBD Dauntless

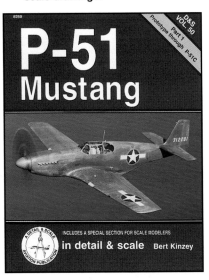

8250 P-51 Mustang Pt 1

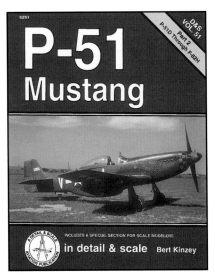

8251 P-51 Mustang Pt 2

8252 SB2C Helldiver

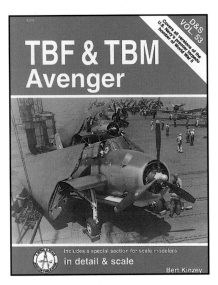

8253 TBF&TBM Avenger

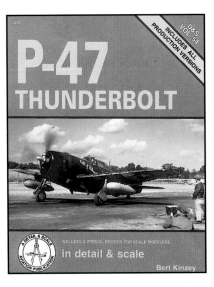

8254 P-47 Thunderbolt

8255 F4U Corsair Pt 1

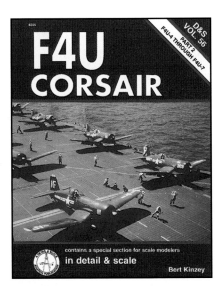

8256 F4U Corsair Pt 2

from squadron/signal publications